FRANCIS FRITH'S

BASILDON LIVING M

THE FRANCIS FRITH COLLECTION

www.francisfrith.com

photographs of the mid twentieth century

Francis Frith's

BASILDON
LIVING MEMORIES

Russell Thompson

First published in the United Kingdom in 2002 by
The Francis Frith Collection

Paperback Edition 2002
ISBN 1-85937-515-4

British Library Cataloguing in Publication Data

Francis Frith's Basildon Living Memories
Russell Thompson

The Francis Frith Collection
Frith's Barn, Teffont,
Salisbury, Wiltshire SP3 5QP
Tel: +44 (0) 1722 716 376
Email: info@francisfrith.co.uk
www.francisfrith.com

Printed and bound in Great Britain

Front Cover: Basildon, Market Place 1961 B438040t

The colour-tinting is for illustrative purposes only, and is not intended to be historically accurate

AS WITH ANY HISTORICAL DATABASE THE FRITH ARCHIVE IS CONSTANTLY BEING CORRECTED AND IMPROVED
AND THE PUBLISHERS WOULD WELCOME INFORMATION ON OMISSIONS OR INACCURACIES

contents

Francis Frith: Victorian Pioneer

FRANCIS FRITH, Victorian founder of the world-famous photographic archive, was a complex and multi-talented man. A devout Quaker and a highly successful Victorian businessman, he was both philosophic by nature and pioneering in outlook.

By 1855 Francis Frith had already established a wholesale grocery business in Liverpool, and sold it for the astonishing sum of £200,000, which is the equivalent today of over £15,000,000. Now a multi-millionaire, he was able to indulge his passion for travel. As a child he had pored over travel books written by early explorers, and his fancy and imagination had been stirred by family holidays to the sublime mountain regions of Wales and Scotland. 'What a land of spirit-stirring and enriching scenes and places!' he had written. He was to return to these scenes of grandeur in later years to 'recapture the thousands of vivid and tender memories', but with a different purpose. Now in his thirties, and captivated by the new science of photography, Frith set out on a series of pioneering journeys to the Nile regions that occupied him from 1856 until 1860.

Intrigue and Adventure

He took with him on his travels a specially-designed wicker carriage that acted as both dark-room and sleeping chamber. These far-flung journeys were packed with intrigue and adventure. In his life story, written when he was sixty-three, Frith tells of being held captive by bandits, and of fighting 'an awful midnight battle to the very point of surrender with a deadly pack of hungry, wild dogs'. Sporting flowing Arab costume, Frith arrived at Akaba by camel seventy years before Lawrence, where he encountered 'desert princes and rival sheikhs, blazing with jewel-hilted swords'.

During these extraordinary adventures he was assiduously exploring the desert regions bordering the Nile and patiently recording the antiquities and peoples with his camera. He was the first photographer to venture beyond the sixth cataract. Africa was still the mysterious 'Dark Continent', and Stanley and Livingstone's historic meeting was a decade into the future. The conditions for picture taking confound belief. He laboured for hours in his wicker dark-room in the sweltering heat of the desert, while the volatile chemicals fizzed dangerously in their trays. Often he was forced to work in remote tombs and caves where conditions were cooler. Back in London he exhibited his photographs and was 'rapturously cheered' by members of the Royal Society. His reputation as a photographer was made overnight. An eminent modern historian has likened their impact on the population of the time to that on our own generation of the first photographs taken on the surface of the moon.

Venture of a Life-Time

Characteristically, Frith quickly spotted the opportunity to create a new business as a specialist publisher of photographs. He lived in an era of immense and sometimes violent change. For the poor in the early part of Victoria's reign work was a drudge and the hours long, and people had precious little free time to enjoy themselves. Most had no transport other than a cart or gig at their disposal, and had not travelled far beyond the boundaries of their own town or village. However,

by the 1870s, the railways had threaded their way across the country, and Bank Holidays and half-day Saturdays had been made obligatory by Act of Parliament. All of a sudden the ordinary working man and his family were able to enjoy days out and see a little more of the world.

With characteristic business acumen, Francis Frith foresaw that these new tourists would enjoy having souvenirs to commemorate their days out. In 1860 he married Mary Ann Rosling and set out with the intention of photographing every city, town and village in Britain. For the next thirty years he travelled the country by train and by pony and trap, producing fine photographs of seaside resorts and beauty spots that were keenly bought by millions of Victorians. These prints were painstakingly pasted into family albums and pored over during the dark nights of winter, rekindling precious memories of summer excursions.

The Rise of Frith & Co

Frith's studio was soon supplying retail shops all over the country. To meet the demand he gathered about him a small team of photographers, and published the work of independent artist-photographers of the calibre of Roger Fenton and Francis Bedford. In order to gain some understanding of the scale of Frith's business one only has to look at the catalogue issued by Frith & Co in 1886: it runs to some 670 pages, listing not only many thousands of views of the British Isles but also many photographs of most European countries, and China, Japan, the USA and Canada – note the sample page shown above from the hand-written *Frith & Co* ledgers detailing pictures taken. By 1890 Frith had created the greatest specialist photographic publishing company in the

world, with over 2,000 outlets – more than the combined number that Boots and W H Smith have today! The picture on the right shows the *Frith & Co* display board at Ingleton in the Yorkshire Dales. Beautifully constructed with mahogany frame and gilt inserts, it could display up to a dozen local scenes.

Postcard Bonanza

The ever-popular holiday postcard we know today took many years to develop. In 1870 the Post Office issued the first plain cards, with a pre-printed stamp on one face. In 1894 they allowed other publishers' cards to be sent through the mail with an attached adhesive halfpenny stamp. Demand grew rapidly, and in 1895 a new size of postcard was permitted called the court card, but there was little room for illustration. In 1899,

a year after Frith's death, a new card measuring 5.5 x 3.5 inches became the standard format, but it was not until 1902 that the divided back came into being, with address and message on one face and a full-size illustration on the other. *Frith & Co* were in the vanguard of postcard development, and Frith's sons Eustace and Cyril continued their father's monumental task, expanding the number of views offered to the public and recording more and more places in Britain, as the coasts and countryside were opened up to mass travel.

Francis Frith died in 1898 at his villa in Cannes, his great project still growing. The archive he created continued in business for another seventy years. By 1970 it contained over a third of a million pictures of 7,000 cities, towns and villages. The massive photographic record Frith has left to us stands as a living monument to a special and very remarkable man.

Frith's Archive: A Unique Legacy

FRANCIS FRITH'S legacy to us today is of immense significance and value, for the magnificent archive of evocative photographs he created provides a unique record of change in 7,000 cities, towns and villages throughout Britain over a century and more. Frith and his fellow studio photographers revisited locations many times down the years to update their views, compiling for us an enthralling and colourful pageant of British life and character.

We tend to think of Frith's sepia views of Britain as nostalgic, for most of us use them to conjure up memories of places in our own lives with which we have family associations. It often makes us forget that to Francis Frith they were records of daily life as it was actually being lived in the cities, towns and villages of his day. The Victorian age was one of great and often bewildering change for ordinary people, and though the pictures evoke an impression of slower times, life was as busy and hectic as it is today.

We are fortunate that Frith was a photographer of the people, dedicated to recording the minutiae of everyday life. For it is this sheer wealth of visual data, the painstaking chronicle of changes in dress, transport, street layouts, buildings, housing, engineering and landscape that captivates us so much today. His remarkable images offer us a powerful link with the past and with the lives of our ancestors.

Today's Technology

Computers have now made it possible for Frith's many thousands of images to be accessed almost instantly. In the Frith archive today, each photograph is carefully 'digitised' then stored on a CD Rom. Frith archivists can locate a single photograph amongst thousands within seconds. Views can be catalogued and sorted under a variety of categories of place and content to the immediate benefit of researchers.

Inexpensive reference prints can be created for them at the touch of a mouse button, and a wide range of books and other printed materials assembled and published for a wider, more general readership - in the next twelve months over a hundred Frith local history titles will be published! The day-to-day workings of the archive are very different from how they were in Francis Frith's time: imagine the herculean task of sorting through eleven tons of glass negatives as Frith had to do to locate a particular sequence of pictures!

See Frith at **www.francisfrith.com**

Yet the archive still prides itself on maintaining the same high standards of excellence laid down by Francis Frith, including the painstaking cataloguing and indexing of every view.

It is curious to reflect on how the internet now allows researchers in America and elsewhere greater instant access to the archive than Frith himself ever enjoyed. Many thousands of individual views can be called up on screen within seconds on one of the Frith internet sites, enabling people living continents away to revisit the streets of their ancestral home town, or view places in Britain where they have enjoyed holidays. Many overseas researchers welcome the chance to view special theme selections, such as transport, sports, costume and ancient monuments.

We are certain that Francis Frith would have heartily approved of these modern developments in imaging techniques, for he himself was always working at the very limits of Victorian photographic technology.

The Value of the Archive Today

Because of the benefits brought by the computer, Frith's images are increasingly studied by social historians, by researchers into genealogy and ancestory, by architects, town planners, and by teachers and schoolchildren involved in local history projects.

In addition, the archive offers every one of us an opportunity to examine the places where we and our families have lived and worked down the years. Highly successful in Frith's own era, the archive is now, a century and more on, entering a new phase of popularity.

The Past in Tune with the Future

Historians consider the Francis Frith Collection to be of prime national importance. It is the only archive of its kind remaining in private ownership and has been valued at a million pounds. However, this figure is now rapidly increasing as digital technology enables more and more people around the world to enjoy its benefits.

Francis Frith's archive is now housed in an historic timber barn in the beautiful village of Teffont in Wiltshire. Its founder would not recognize the archive office as it is today. In place of the many thousands of dusty boxes containing glass plate negatives and an all-pervading odour of photographic chemicals, there are now ranks of computer screens. He would be amazed to watch his images travelling round the world at unimaginable speeds through network and internet lines.

The archive's future is both bright and exciting. Francis Frith, with his unshakeable belief in making photographs available to the greatest number of people, would undoubtedly approve of what is being done today with his lifetime's work. His photographs, depicting our shared past, are now bringing pleasure and enlightenment to millions around the world a century and more after his death.

Basildon Living Memories
An Introduction

Destruction and regeneration are common themes. They occur in several mythologies - the Biblical flood and the Germanic Twilight of the Gods are examples that spring readily to mind. The context is generally the same: an old world, having become unworkable, is destroyed by water or fire and replaced by a gleaming new Utopia. In mythology, it is all very clear-cut. Everything is black, white, green or gold.

It is improbable that Teutonic myth was foremost in the mind of the Rt Hon Lewis Silkin, Minister of Town & Country Planning, as he stood in Laindon High Road School one October night in 1948. Nevertheless, there were parallels. The old world was a sprawl of cottages and sheds - dwellings that were being described as 'sub-standard'. The deluge, if it came, would not be of fire and water, but of mud and, many predicted, tears. The Minister was in Laindon to persuade the town's understandably horrified freeholders to sacrifice their homes for a better, brighter future. In fairness, no-one had expected his task to be an easy one.

Basildon has an unusual history. The majority of towns just seem to happen. Of course, they are subject to changes in economics, technology, geography, and the social climate; but change is seldom wholesale. The town we now call Basildon, however, is rather different, in that it was created very deliberately. And it happened not once, but twice.

At the start of the 19th century, Basildon was a small parish with a negligible population. It was bounded on the west by Laindon, Dunton, Langdon Hills and Lee Chapel; on the south and east by Vange, Pitsea and Nevendon. All were quiet, agricultural places - but those days were numbered.

The problem lay in the stodgy London clay that characterises this part of Essex. Always a devil to plough, the farmers used to call it 'three horse land'. Cheap grain was starting to be imported from America, and what with some poor harvests in the 1870s, an agricultural depression was soon underway in England. The writing, it seemed, was on the barn wall.

Land was being put to new uses. Out on the coast, farming and fishing villages were reinventing themselves as new-fangled watering-places. Southend was Essex's prime example. There had been a meandering railway line connecting Southend to London since the 1850s, but it was the building of a second, more direct line that affects our story. Completed in 1889, it cut straight across the Basildon area, re-joining the older line at Pitsea Junction.

With south-east Essex suddenly accessible, and farmland falling out of cultivation, something was bound to happen. It did. From 1885 onwards, land-agents had been acquiring the disused fields and offering them for sale as building land. After a few false starts, they hit upon the idea of carving the land into minuscule plots, roughly 18 ft wide, and offering them to buyers of fairly limited means. These early plots tended to centre on the stations at Laindon and Pitsea. Advertisements appeared at strategic points around London, many of them stressing the hygienic nature of the countryside: 'Laindon - a lovely, lofty locality, loved by Londoners ... Rejuvenating rural residence', declared one alliteration-fixated leaflet.

The land-agents subsidised the rail fares of interested parties, and filled them with food and alcohol as soon as they stepped off the train. For this reason, the plots became known as 'champagne estates'. Many of the customers were poor East Londoners, who could not have afforded to buy a plot even if they had wished

to. They just wanted a day out. Several of them did buy plots - under the influence - and never returned.

To stress the negative angle, however, is to do a disservice to the thousands of people who, over the next six decades, made the plotlands their home. The sales continued after the First World War, and the heyday of these rough-and-ready freeholdings was to occur in the 1920s and 30s. At first, the plotlands had simply been intended as weekend retreats for weary Londoners. Families would pitch a bell-tent on their patch of land. Gradually, however, they got the building instinct, and would arrive on Friday nights with a barrow-load of timber. Bizarre townships of shacks and bungalows began sprouting up like mushrooms. Often a railway carriage or a London bus would find its way onto a plot, and metamorphose into somebody's home. With the depression of the 1920s, these first-time builders were unable to afford luxuries such as bricks. They often resorted to corrugated iron and asbestos sheeting - anything that came to hand. Nevertheless, people had begun to actually live in their constructions, and to commute to work. Basic though the accommodation was, it was often better than whatever London rookery they had left behind them. Maybe the advertisements were true: perhaps Pitsea was, indeed, 'picturesque' and Laindon 'lovely'.

As the estates grew, so did the villages themselves:

Laindon High Road became a continuous string of shops, as did the London Road at Vange and Pitsea. In terms of other amenities, however, progress was slow: mains water, for instance, was out of the question for most plotland dwellings. And, whilst some of the inhabitants clubbed together and solidified their roadways with duckboards, cinders, or (very occasionally) concrete, many roads were never more than grass tracks - wild in summer, abominable in winter.

During the Second World War, some of the unsold plots returned to agricultural purposes. The plotlanders, meanwhile, had become a permanent fixture, despite the flimsy nature of their homes. By the end of the 1940s, the population of Laindon-Pitsea was 25,000. The local authority, Billericay Urban District Council, was concerned about the lack of facilities in the area, but could simply not afford to give this big, sprawling settlement the makeover it so urgently needed.

Anyway, south-east England had more immediate problems. East London had suffered badly during the recent bombing raids. 20,000 people had lost their homes in East and West Ham alone. Something had to be done for them: new starts, and - if necessary - new towns. Sure enough, the New Towns Act was passed in 1946, and the search began for suitable locations. Stevenage, Crawley, Harlow ... all became names to conjure

with. Billericay UDC must have thought it was Christmas: here was an opportunity to re-plan and rebuild on a major scale, and furthermore, the government would foot the bill. The Council were consequently unique in actually asking to be considered as the site for a New Town. The government liked the idea: after all, because of the plotlands, Laindon and Pitsea already had strong links with East London. The scheme was given official approval in May 1948, and the Minister for Town & Country Planning was sent, in due course, to explain the situation to the freeholders.

The Laindon Residents' Protection Association had sprung into life as soon as the news leaked out. For years, the freeholders had poured all their hopes, resources and time into what was now being described as a 'shanty town'. They were going to fight these proposals every step of the way. However, Basildon New Town's story is, as we know, a story of the little guy taking on the big corporation - and losing. Indeed, a vast number of residents welcomed the New Town with open arms. And who could blame them? There would be electric lighting, brick walls and flushing toilets.

Basildon Development Corporation was formed by the Department of the Environment in order to manage the New Town. They had a mountain to climb: the designated area was in roughly 30,000 ownerships. There were 1,300 acres of

wasteland, of which half had no traceable owner. This was still causing headaches into the 1980s, as long-lost contracts turned up and descendants of would-be plotlanders tried to claim their inheritance. Some of the established freeholders did not go gently - barricading themselves inside their homes, or clambering onto their roofs with shotguns. 'Basildon was built on tears' became a familiar observation.

In any case, Basildon could not be built overnight. With an original target of 50,000 people living in 15 self-contained 'neighbourhoods', it would take time. An area between Laindon and Pitsea, not far from the old village of Basildon, had been selected as the centre of the New Town. But how could business and industry be attracted to an as-yet non-existent town? How could the freeholders be integrated with the incoming population?

The Development Corporation spent the next 37 years building houses. Several of the sites earmarked for development were saved by conservationists, much to their credit. It was not until 1986 that the Development Corporation was disbanded.

There had been mistakes, naturally. The wholesale demolition of almost all the area's ancient houses and farms now seems scandalous. There were human problems too, such as the 'Basildon blues' that afflicted some of the new settlers when they found themselves on half-built housing estates in the middle of nowhere. Where were the shops? The entertainments? Why did this New Town have no hospital or central railway station?

In many ways, Basildon's story is the story of the 20th century. All across the country, people were having changes thrust upon them by forces that were outside their control. They were understandably eager to claw back whatever they could, and make some tangible, attainable changes of their own. The Rt Hon Lewis Silkin knew that. When he stood and faced Laindon's freeholders in 1948, he used words like 'civilisation', 'knowledge' and 'community' - big things. Ideals. For decades, Basildon had been about small-scale, home-made things. But there was a wider world out there, and it was changing.

Outside it was already dark. Slowly, though, the second half of the 20th century was stirring into life.

◀ **Langdon Hills
The Park Entrance
and Keeper's Cottage
c1950** L151005
One Tree Hill and
Westley Heights were
together designated
Langdon Hills Country
Park in 1973. The
County Council had
been buying parcels of
land in this area since
the 1930s, in an attempt
to preserve the native
trees. Whitebeam,
Turkey oak, beech,
poplar, sycamore and
alder abound here.

Langdon Hills & Laindon

◄ **Corringham, One Tree Hill c1955** C243048
Formerly Bennitts Hill, One Tree Hill was named after the large ash that stood here until the First World War (when it blew down in a gale). It had once proved a useful landmark for shipping on the Thames. In 1926, a mineral well was discovered in Martinhole Wood, just below the hill.

◄ **Langdon Hills The Crown Hotel c1960** L150029
Crown Hill was the setting for an unusual wager in 1936: a Grays confectioner was bet that he could not cycle backwards up the 1-in-7 road. He did it - twice - even though his challenger failed to show up. The Crown is a 200-year-old pub that once hosted 'smoking concerts'. The plasterwork crown above the entrance is dated 1874.

Langdon Hills, Westley Road c1950
L151004
After the First World War, there were plans to divide Westley Heights into 231 small plots of land and offer them for development. There was a public outcry, however, and the County Council bought the land as Open Space in 1932. Westley, or West Lee, was once a parish in its own right (Lee Chapel being 'East Lee'). Its church is thought to have stood somewhere in the vicinity of Westley Hall.

Langdon Hills, High Road c1950 L151001
Famously the second-highest point in Essex (the highest being a patch of undistinguished woodland in the parish of Langley), Langdon Hills certainly impressed the traveller Arthur Young. 'Nothing can exceed it', he wrote, 'except that which Hannibal exhibited to his disconsolate troops when he bade them behold the glories of the Italian plains!'

Langdon Hills, High Road c1950
L151002
The plotland development of this part of Basildon stemmed from the agricultural depression of the 1870s. Initially focused on Laindon station, it soon engulfed parts of Langdon Hills and Dunton. The hilliness of these parishes was often equated with 'Pure Air and Good Health' in the property advertisements.

Langdon Hills, High Road c1950
L151003
Harry Bebington was the first chairman of Billericay Urban District Council (established 1934). He was also a land-agent, who sold plots at Laindon and Langdon Hills for £5 a time. His office can be seen here, at the corner of Berry Lane. The High Road itself, ironically, tended to be where the better-quality homes were built.

Laindon, King Edward Road c1960 ▶ L150031
The grid-like pattern of the streets west of Laindon High Road preserves the layout of some of the early plotland estates. The tarmac, however, is a far cry from the 'wilderness of slime and ooze' that once characterised these side-roads. Some of the street names capture the spirit of the age: King Edward, New Century, Victoria.

◀ **Laindon, The School c1955** L150008
Laindon School - formerly Laindon High Road School - opened in 1928. It eventually merged with Nicholas School to become the new James Hornby High School (named after the final teacher at the St Nicholas's church annexe). The Laindon site was finally closed in 2000, when it was decided that the Nicholas buildings were more suitable.

◄ **Laindon, The Fortune of War Hotel c1960** L150033
After a spell as the Hustlers, this pub has reverted to its original name. Opened in 1928, it replaced a previous Fortune of War (now a printer's on the Billericay road), which had itself been founded, supposedly, by a soldier returning from the Napoleonic Wars. At the time of our photo, the pub offered 'dancing every Friday, Saturday and Sunday evening - to the music of the Roundabouts'. In view of the pub's position on the arterial road, the band were aptly named.

◄ Laindon, View from St Nicholas's Church c1955 L150030

We are looking north-east, towards Botney Hill at Little Burstead. The long fields in the middle distance were filled with houses soon after this picture was taken, with the development of the Basildon Drive estate. Laindon churchyard still remains a surprisingly wild and tranquil place.

◄ **Laindon, St Nicholas's Church c1955** L150035
Laindon church boasts one of Essex's famous timber belfries. The annexe to the left of the belfry is a 17th-century priest's house, which later became a school. It was known as Puckle's School, after a landowner who in 1614 bequeathed all his land to the church. This endowment paid for the teacher's wages.

▼ **Laindon, Church Road c1955** L150016
The bungalows along Church Road are fairly representative of the kind of housing to be seen in Laindon before the New Town came. Several of them are still there. At the top of the street, Church Road was already bisected by the arterial road to Southend.

◄ **Laindon, The Cross Roads c1955** L150015
The A127 arterial road (in the foreground) was opened in 1925 by Prince Henry, and succeeded Wash Road as the main east-west route through Laindon. When the New Town was developed, it was realised that the arterial would limit the town's northward spread. Note the 'Cyclists Only' sign in the photo: cycle paths are by no means a recent idea.

Laindon, Wash Road c1955 L150012
Wash Road was a road of many farms: Watch-House, Mundell's, Petchey's, Benson's, Puckle's, Sellers, and Laindonponds. The first-named is just out of shot, beyond the bungalows, though several of the others have gone. The wash itself - near Laindonponds - was where a tributary of the Crouch forded the road.

Laindon, Wash Road
c1955 L150011
D & E Flack's (left) was a general store and post office serving the area north of the Southend road. By the end of the 1950s, outlying shops were competing with the new Town Centre development. Reckitts Blue - advertised on the fence - was a well-known bleaching agent of the time.

▼ Laindon, Martindale Avenue
c1955 L150013
Martindale Avenue predates the New Town. The 1920s and 30s had been something of a boom time for Laindon, though many observers were less than enamoured with the 'eruption of villas and bungalows' that sprang up around this time. Today, this particular avenue is unchanged - if slightly more potholed.

◄ Laindon, Wash Road
c1955 L150014
The original Prince of Wales pub was a simple-looking 17th-century structure. It was rebuilt in a suitably gung-ho style in the 1930s (centre left). The land opposite the pub is now occupied by housing and a recreation-ground, whilst the house with the appealingly rickety weatherboarding has been dismantled.

Basildon Town Centre

Market Place 1961 B438040
Basildon's market opened on 6 September 1958. The caravan on the left is the Basildon School of Motoring's mobile office; the one on the right is a fish stall, offering skate, crabs, live eels and 'new season Scotch kippers - full of oil'. The ladies' calf-length, wide-collared coats are typical of the era.

Market Pavement c1965 B438070
Basildon's first shop opened in Market Pavement on 16 August 1958. It was the premises of Allan Henbest, a tailor and outfitter, formerly of Laindon High Road. He was a well-known local figure, but unfortunately that did not help him when he found himself competing with the chain-stores that followed him into the town centre.

Market Place 1961 B438011a
The town centre was constructed on a plateau halfway between Laindon and Vange. The block of 41 shops facing Market Square was the first to be built. The butcher's, nearest the camera, is certainly attracting window-shoppers. Just to its left is a cafeteria.

Market Place 1961 B438003
This is an interesting scene showing the clean, young New Town. A large proportion of the settlers were young themselves - look at the number of children and pushchairs here. Everything bears the hallmarks of the late 1950s and early 60s - from the contours of the ice-cream van (right) to the Guinness advertisement (with the shoe-soles) on the hoarding (centre left).

The Clock c1965 B438019a
Basildon's spherical clock remains an impressive example of 1960s design, but it has been superseded by
Rowland Emmett's 'Pussiewillow III' clock outside SavaCentre. Installed in 1980, this contraption whirrs, whirls
and plays music every fifteen minutes - it also tells the time.

▼ The Clock c1965 B438024

The church of St Martin le Tours, on the right, was consecrated in 1962. The clump of trees just in front of it marks the position of Barstable Cottage, one of the thousands of small tenements swept away by the New Town. It was entirely wooden apart from its chimney-stack. The Development Corporation bought it from the owners for £150.

▼ The Town Square c1965 B438023

Brooke House, the town centre's only housing unit, opened on 7 July 1962. A 14-storey block of 84 flats, it was named after Henry Brooke, the former Housing Minister. The Town Square itself had begun to take shape by 1958, with the development of the shops on the left (incorporating Sainsbury's, Boots and Woolworth's).

▲ The Town Square c1965
B438020
Keay House - on the right - was home to Basildon Urban District Council from 1960 to 1965. It took its name from Sir Lancelot Keay, the first chairman of Basildon Development Corporation. Its mural of bold primary colours was the work of the artist Anthony Holloway, and allegedly had no 'title, meaning or message'.

◄ **The Statue 1961** B438001
Maurice Lambert's 'Mother and Child' was commissioned in 1959, as a symbol of the New Town's growth. The growth is self-evident here, with Brooke House's massive V-shaped struts in the background (left), and the post office under construction. Lambert spent a year on the sculpture; Basildon spent £4,000 on it.

South Gunnels c1965 ▶
B438028

Before the construction of the town centre, there were few shops in the new Basildon. Initially, just two small Co-ops served the first few hundred inhabitants in the Fryerns neighbourhood. It was quite a while before a more all-encompassing parade was built. Mobile traders thrived in the intervening period.

◀ The Town Square c1965 B438025

This is a good study of the stark angularity favoured by 1960s architects. The children's clothing, too, is characteristic of the time. The 'Mother and Child' sculpture, behind the children, now forms part of Basildon's logo, such has been the extent to which people associate it with the town.

◄ **East Square c1965**
B438327
The post office was
opened in 1963.
There were around
160 shops in the town
centre by this time,
and the Development
Corporation had
turned their attention
to providing Basildon
with a health centre,
and also police, fire and
ambulance stations. The
long-delayed hospital
was not ready until
1973.

**Freedom House
c1965** B438026
Freedom House was
built by 1960. At the
time of our photo, its
three echelons included
ABC Wallpapers,
Forbuoys newsagents
and Robinson Rentals
at the bottom; Peter's
gents' hairdressing
and Hart's store in the
middle; and offices
for estate agents and
chartered surveyors at
the top.

The View from Freedom House c1965 B438066
Work on the town centre had begun in 1956. The shops at Laindon, Vange and Pitsea - the old centres - tended to suffer as new business was drawn into the precinct. In the 1930s, Laindon High Road had consisted of 120 shops; only one of the old buildings now remains.

East Walk c1965
B438015
Although Basildon was burgeoning as a commercial centre, the presence of the Bankrupt Stock Clearance shop on the right indicates that not everybody was doing well. It was always intended that Basildon would become a Mecca for regional shopping - an aim that was realised when the famous Eastgate Shopping Centre opened in 1985.

East Walk c1965

B438014

Old-fashioned, coach-built prams were still very much in evidence in 1965, though they were gradually rendered redundant as car ownership increased and foldaway buggies came into their own. The original plan for Basildon, however, was for each neighbourhood to have its principal amenities within easy walking distance.

Southernhay c1965 ▶
B438305

The town centre was extended eastwards in the 1980s, and Southernhay was diverted. This stretch of the road survives as a walkway in the precinct. Gina Murray's hairdressing salon, on the far left, offered 'Permanent Waving from 21/-. Satisfaction Guaranteed'. Triumph Heralds and Ford Consuls were the cars of the day.

◀ **Detail From: Southernhay c1965** B438305

The Bus Station c1965
B438330

The bus station managed to combine functionalism with aesthetics. The mosaic along its fascia measures 315×13ft, and consists of 16,000 hand-printed tiles. The artist was John Gordon. Buses were seen as a vital conduit to and from the new estates: they ran at a frequency that compares very favourably with today's timetables.

Blenheim House and the Bus Terminus 1961 B438015a

Blenheim House contained the Locarno (later Tiffany's Ballroom), where the resident group in the early 1960s were the pre-fame Dave Clark Five. Contemporaneous fashions undoubtedly included the Mekay 'immaculate shirts' advertised on the side of the 244 bus (which served Whitmore Way and Laindon).

The Bus Station c1965 B438029a

The bus station was built to incorporate a parade of shops, seen here beneath the canopy. By the mid 1960s, dress sensibilities were changing: the young woman in Bay A is wearing a mini-skirt, whilst the man in Bay B sports narrow jeans. His companion is evidently a clippie (see her ticket-machine) - a breed that is now extinct outside metropolitan areas.

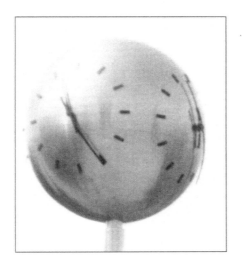

Details from: The Clock c1965 B438019a **East Walk c1965** B438015
East Walk c1965 B438014 **& The Town Square c1965** B438020a

In the Neighbourhoods

Long Riding c1960 B438007
The Basildon Development Corporation aimed at providing a wide range of different types of housing - both for visual reasons, and also to attract residents from different income-groups. Maisonettes, terraces, semis, bungalows, flats and detached houses all had a place in the new neighbourhoods.

◀ **Whitmore Way 1961**
B438027
The early neighbourhoods were characterised by winding streets and plenty of open space. Some of the plans won awards. Whitmore Way was the site of Basildon's first proper shopping parade: this included a chemist, a hardware shop, a post office, a Martin's newsagent, a Home & Colonial store, and a much-needed chip-shop.

Long Riding c1960
B438006
8,336 new homes had been built in Basildon by 1960. One problem not foreseen by the planners was the dramatic increase in car ownership. The initial blueprint allowed for one garage for every six homes. Come 1957, the ratio had been lowered to 1:2, and soon became 1:1.

The Jolly Friar c1960   B438005
It was planned that each neighbourhood in the New Town would have its own pub. The first to materialise was the Crane (taking its name from the demolished Cranes Farm) in Pendle Drive on the Fryerns estate. The Jolly Friar was built nearby in Whitmore Way. The oldest pub surviving in the New Town area is the Five Bells at Vange.

The Industrial Estate c1965
B438034
Basildon's first new factory, South East Essex Wholesale Dairies, opened in 1951. Over the next two years, the No 1 Industrial Estate sprang up around it. The dominant building was the Carreras Rothman factory (in the distance, with the clock). It closed in 1984, costing Basildon 1,500 jobs. Fifteen years earlier, it had been producing 65% of all the cigarettes exported from Britain. Amongst its innovations had been 'fat filter cigarettes, luxury length menthol cigarettes, double filters and charcoal filters'.

The Industrial Estate c1965 B438031
The Ford Tractor Plant - resplendent with its 600,000 gallon water-tower (right) - occupied the whole of the No 3 Industrial Estate. Built in the mid 1950s, it was followed into the town by the Ford Engineering Research Centre at Dunton. When it was taken over by the New Holland Machinery Company in 1994, the plant had manufactured 1,347,000 tractors.

The Industrial Estate c1965 B438332
Basildon's original target was that 16,000 people should be employed on its industrial estates. This picture shows the No 2 Industrial Estate, with Gloucester Park to the right. Wass, Pritchard & Co, in the foreground, were printers, specialising in holiday brochures, catalogues, foreign stamps, and wrappers for chocolates and razor-blades.

◄ **Ghyllgrove c1960**
B438030
A number of neighbourhoods - Fryerns, Barstable, Kingswood and Lee Chapel South - were in place by 1958. Then, the government issued plans for increased house-building all over the country. The south-west corner of the proposed Gloucester Park was therefore set aside for the Ghyllgrove neighbourhood.

Woodlands Girls' School c1960 B438033
A shake-up in the mid 1960s saw mergers between several Basildon schools. Amongst other things, this spelt the end of the town's two highly-regarded grammar-technical schools, Fryerns and Barstable. The Minister of Education, however, was keen that Woodlands Girls' and Boys' Schools should remain segregated.

Woodlands Boys' School c1960 B438032 Beyond the playing field, we can see some of the Kingswood neighbourhood's dormy-style houses. These were the first 'quality' private homes to be built in the new Basildon. The two Woodlands Schools were combined in 1978.

Kingswood County Primary School c1960
B438038
At first, Basildon's schools were insufficient to house the surge of New Towners. For some of the primary-age children, there were places in existing schools at Vange and Pitsea. Other pupils were shuttled to schools in Benfleet. Basildon's first new school - Swan Mead Junior & Infants, in Church Road - opened in April 1954. Kingswood was built soon after.

The View from Vange Hall c1960 B438002 We are standing on what is now the golf course, above The Dell and Swallowdale. In the distance, right of centre, is the long, pale form of the recently-completed Keay House. The 16th-century Vange Hall stood a little way to our right, near what is thought to have been the site of a Roman brickworks. All that now remains of the Hall is its duck pond.

◄ **Pitsea, The View from the Church c1955** P145024
Pitsea Hall Island - to the left of the creek - has a complex history. Originally pasture and arable land, it was taken over by British Explosives Ltd in 1890. The earthen banks of several protective blast-barriers still pockmark the site. They were no help, sadly, to the three men who died in an explosion here in 1913. During the First World War, the area was used as a storage depot by troopships, and later became a rather controversial refuse-tip. It began a new life as Wat Tyler Country Park in 1984.

Pitsea and Beyond

◄ **Pitsea, St Michael's Church c1955** P145002
The late 20th century was not kind to St Michael's. It was still in use in the early 1970s, but it was later abandoned and fell prey to vandals. The nave and chancel were finally demolished in December 1998. The 15th-century tower was spared, and now serves a new religion: it supports a mobile phone mast.

◄ **Pitsea, The View from the Church c1955** P145045
The northward view is slightly less romantic: Pitsea High Road crosses the centre of the picture, with the Northlands estate behind it. The building that was originally the Railway Tavern is hidden by the tall tree on the right. Its mock-Tudor successor can be seen to the left.

◄ **Pitsea, The Broadway c1955** P145027
Harold George Howard's first row of shops appeared in 1929. It included the cinema, still known as the Broadway here, but later renamed the Century. It boasted a café serving 'luncheons, teas, suppers'. The cinema closed in 1969 (the year that also saw the closure of Pitsea's original market - another fondly-remembered institution).

◄ Pitsea, High Road c1955
P145040

In the late 1920s, Harold George Howard, a prosperous dairy-farmer, drew up plans for a new Pitsea. The Railway Hotel and two blocks of Tudor-style shops were built, but Howard's vision was scuppered by the Second World War. His buildings survived the coming of the New Town, however, and his name is preserved in Howard Park and Howard Crescent.

▼ Pitsea, The Memorial c1955 P145043

The original Railway Tavern dated from 1859. The building was later transformed into shops, but has now gone. Its replacement, the Railway Hotel that we see here, was built between the wars at the Station Lane junction. The pub became especially well-known for its home-cooked hams. The war memorial - with Greek maiden and her once fully-operational electric torch - had been erected in 1922. When this area became a tortuous gyratory system, she was shifted to Howard Park.

◄ Pitsea, Plotlands c1955
P145011

This is one of the unmade roads to the west of Rectory Road - perhaps Hillcrest Chase or Rectory Park Drive. St Michael's church looms in the background. This bungaloid development was typical of Pitsea in pre-New Town days. Such roads were, at best, basic in their amenities, but were generally much-loved by their residents.

Pitsea, St Michael's Church Hall c1955 P145012
The church hall, in Rectory Road, was much more central to Pitsea than the medieval church, perched on its hilltop site. The church halls of Basildon played a major role in providing activities for the swelling population. A new church, St Gabriel's, opened in Rectory Road in the 1960s.

Pitsea, Rectory Road c1955 P145010a
This parade was built in the years prior to the Second World War, as Pitsea's houses began to inch along Rectory Road. On the left stands Chalvedon Stores, with its bulky 1930s delivery-van and adverts for Whitbread's beer. Its neighbours include The Cabin newsagents, and a second-hand furniture shop.

Pitsea, Rectory Road c1955 P145019
Rectory Road was extensively redeveloped in
the 1970s, and many of its small shops were
closed. John Shore's shored-up grocery-store
is here advertising Spratt's Dog & Bird Foods,
Player's, Nevill's Bread, and Oxo ('For Cooking
& Drinking').

◄ **Pitsea, Gun Hill c1955**
P145047
Gun Hill takes its name from the Gun Inn, further up London Road at Bowers Gifford. The pub seen here - the Bull - is displaying a 'Sundays: No Coaches' sign. This was still the main A13 trunk road to the sea, and therefore well-used by day trippers. Behind the inn sign are the buildings of Bull Farm.

◄ Pitsea, High Road c1955
P145051

We are looking west from the Rectory Road corner. The shops on the left were sacrificed when the new A13 cut across Pitsea in the early 1970s. They had included, at various times, S C Jones the newsagent (with the patriotic window-display, left) and Starling's the ironmonger's (with the gable). On the right is W Norton's antique shop.

▼ Bowers Gifford, The Basildon Development Corporation c1960 B438039

The Development Corporation was formed in January 1949, with a view to converting the area into a workable New Town. Their headquarters, Gifford House, were just outside the New Town boundaries, a fact that prompted accusations of stand-offishness. Even so, there were suggestions in the 1960s of extending the development zone eastwards. 'I must admit I have often cast lustful eyes on Bowers Gifford's acres which I can see from my office window', said General Manager Charles Boniface.

◄ South Benfleet The Parade c1955
S278032

These days Hopes Green is simply a westward extension of South Benfleet, but it started life as a hamlet of fishermen's cottages. In fact, a navigable creek once brought boats right up to where we are standing (near the entrance to the playing fields). What would the fishermen have made of shops such as Dressywear (left)?

▼ South Benfleet, The Anchor c1960 S278064

The building that later became the Anchor was first erected in 1380. Evidently it was a popular place, since a song was published about it in 1918: 'There's good entertainment for man and beast / At this ancient smuggler's nest ...' At that time, Benfleet's only public transport, a horse and carriage, operated from outside the pub.

▼ South Benfleet, The Creek looking West c1960 S278051

Benfleet Creek has seen its dramas. A Danish invasion fleet arrived here in 893, commanded by the warlord Haesten. His fort seems to have been where the church was subsequently built. The English - under the future King Edward the Elder - stormed the encampment and fired the ships. Charred timbers were found in the 19th century.

▲ South Benfleet, Boyce Hill Golf Links c1955

S278007
Boyce Hill took its name from a medieval land-owning family: their farm stood where the clubhouse now is. Benfleet's wooded hills once provided vital material for fuel and boat-building. Though still fairly well-endowed with trees in the 1950s, the slopes were vanishing under the housing developments of Tarpots and New Thundersley.

◄ **Thundersley
Weir Roundabout c1955**
T113031
The so-called Rayleigh Weir - the source of one of the tributaries of the River Roach - gives its name to this busy junction on the Southend arterial. Here, the Weir Hotel is offering 'Luncheons - Hovis' to the drivers of passing Fords, Austins and Jowett Javelins.

Thundersley
The White Hart and the Shops c1965 T113043
There has been a White Hart in Thundersley since 1797.
Before that, a pub called the Horseshoes had stood nearby,
on the site of Hart Cottages. A forge was located next to
the present Hart until 1958, when it made way for Swans
Green Close and the pub's car-park.

A Circular Tour

Battlesbridge
The River Crouch c1955 W195017
Despite speculation about rampaging Danes, Battlesbridge is actually named after the 14th-century Bataille family. This is now the lowest crossing-point on the Crouch (though bridges once existed at Hullbridge and Fambridge), and at this point the river suddenly ceases to be a modest stream. The bridge itself has had several incarnations - one of which collapsed in the 19th century beneath a 12-ton traction engine. There were once two mills here - one tidal, one steam-rolling - though the place is now best known for its antiques centre.

**Wickford
The High Street c1955**
W195003
We are looking south, towards Halls Corner. The shops on the left were built with bricks from the Nevendon Road brickworks. The shrubs conceal Ladybrow, a former doctor's house and surgery. It was demolished in the late 1960s, and the site is now occupied by the Ladygate Shopping Centre.

◄ **Runwell, The Quart Pot c1955** W195014
Judging by the slogan on the rectory wall, not everyone was happy with the post-war Conservative government. The Quart Pot, a Baddow Brewery house, was where Wickford's Salvation Army had their early meetings. They would apparently leave a copy of the 'War Cry' in the hollow oak outside the pub, for the benefit of passers-by.

Wickford
The Broadway c1955
W195001

Pardey & Johnson traded from the gabled building on the left. Basically a grocery shop and off-licence, it also accommodated Wickford's post office around the time of our picture. The in-store café can be seen to the extreme left. The pub sign a few doors along marks the position of the White Swan.

Crays Hill
The Homestead Café
c1955 C244002

Crays Hill lies equidistant between Wickford and Billericay, its crest just above the 150 ft contour. The thirst-inducing climb meant that there was always food and drink available at various outlets.
This café is the sort of simple building that once proliferated in the Basildon area.

Crays Hill
The Shepherd and Dog
c1955 C244005

The Shepherd & Dog (right) is a 300-year-old pub at the top of the hill. The petrol station still exists in an expanded form. Crays Hill has, in the past, been at the centre of various speculative transport schemes: there was once talk of an Islington-Wallasea railway passing this way, as well as plans to link the village to Purfleet and Battlesbridge by canal.

Crays Hill, London Road c1955
C244009
Hemmings' shopfront is a collage of mid 1950s consumer wares: for the smoker, there are Woodbines, Player's and Gold Flake; for the reader, Picture Post, Home Notes and the Leader. Also available are Spratt's biscuits, Colman's mustard, Corona, and Ledicott's Old Style Ginger Beer. Something for everyone.

Crays Hill, London Road c1955 C244012
Pump Cottage (in the middle of our photo) was - as the name suggests - the source of the village's water-supply. It dates from about 1860. The well pre-dated the cottage by a decade. Crays Hill National School used to stand amongst the trees on the right.

Crays Hill, All Saints' Church c1955 C244001
Crays Hill is a thoroughfare settlement in the parish of Ramsden Crays - the name ultimately coming from the 12th-century de Crei family. With the medieval parish church a mile away, All Saints' was built in a more central position in 1928. It is now a turretless church hall.

Billericay, High Street c1960 B319070
The weatherboarded pair of buildings nearest the camera were once a pub called the Magpie & Horseshoes. The older section (with the bow windows) was built in 1577. It was in the hands of the Bessom family from the early 19th century until 1975. They ran a plumbing and decorating business here in the 20th century. The van belongs to Magee's Nurseries: 'Mushrooms & tomatoes - direct from the garden'.

Billericay, The Chantry Café c1955 B319013
A chantry was established in Billericay in 1342. The Chantry Café probably occupies the site of the priest's house. The building - with the date 1510 on its gable - is reputedly where four local Puritans met before sailing to the New World aboard the Mayflower. There is a Billerica (no 'y') in Massachusetts to this day.

Billericay, High Street c1955 B319079
Several of these buildings are either altered or gone. Bleak House (with the pedimented doorway, right) has been demolished, and rebuilt to an almost identical design. The shop to its immediate left replaced an old house that had been weakened by a detonation during the Second World War. The high-roofed White Hart, along the road, survives to this day.

Billericay, The Roman Catholic Church c1955 B319026
The Church of the Most Holy Redeemer opened in 1919. Its predecessor was St Edith's - a house of Ursuline Sisters at the southern end of the High Street. They celebrated Mass there from 1910 until they left the town three years later. Work began immediately on this new church in Laindon Road.

**West Horndon
Thorndon Avenue
c1965** W189006
This is a quintessentially
mid 1960s scene: a
Ford Anglia, a Mary
Quant haircut, a
cigarette machine.
The Oxfam poster
both pre-empts the
later popularity of
charity-shopping,
and also displays an
effective line in ironic
copywriting. Fading
into the distance is
the high ground of
Thorndon Park.

West Horndon, Dunmow Gardens c1965 W189004
West Horndon is a planned village dating only from the 1940s. Before that, it had been a sparsely-inhabited parish, whose medieval church had collapsed by the early 18th century. The railway station - formerly called East Horndon - stood in the middle of nowhere when it was first built in 1886; the Railway Hotel was previously a coaching inn. West Horndon is now a compact settlement with a small industrial estate, and some good footpaths leading to Bulphan Fen.

Bulphan, Fen Lane c1955 B323004
The second element of Bulphan's name is the word 'fen'. A R Hope Moncrieff, writing in 1909, described Bulphan Fen as 'a flat of woods and pastures that are at worst characteristic, and at the best pleasantly and solitarily rustic'. It is still a world of long, straight field-paths and right-angled lanes.

◄ **Bulphan, The Harrow Inn c1955** B323008
The Harrow stands on the road to North Ockendon. It retains its rural seclusion in spite of recent threats: plans for a major housing development, just north of here at Tillingham Hall, were challenged and overturned in 1987.

◄ **Horndon-on-the-Hill High Street c1960**

H178001

We are facing north, towards Horndon's school. The houses nearest us were once commercial premises - a hardware store and a tailor's. To the right of them lies Swan Meadow, once home to the village fair. This event survives as Horndon-on-the-Hill Feast & Fayre, which takes place at the end of June, to mark St Peter's Day.

◄ **Bulphan, The School c1955** B323007
The National School was built in 1852 to accommodate 70 children. Bulphan was always a smallish village. According to a directory of 1899, it then consisted of a post office, a blacksmith, a grocery shop, a bakery-cum-beer shop, and a few farms.

Horndon-on-the-Hill The Lych-Gate and the Church c1960 H178003 ►
Horndon was once a prosperous wool-town. St Peter and St Paul's church, with its shingled spire and hefty timber belfry, was built in the 13th century. The lych-gate was originally where part of the burial service took place - 'lych' is a medieval word for a corpse.

▲ **Horndon-on-the-Hill Orsett Road c1960** H178005
Horndon has historical footnotes to make it both proud and ashamed. Firstly, the Shaa family, who owned land here, produced two Mayors of London. Secondly, a local farmer called Thomas Higbed was burned at the stake in 1555, on a charge of heresy. He died in his own village, probably in a field opposite the school.

Details from: Corringham Woodbrooke Way c1955 C243044 **Pitsea, Rectory Road c1955** P145019 & **West Horndon Thorndon Avenue c1965** W189006

Horndon-on-the-Hill, High Street c1960 H178006
Horndon's Woolmarket, where the trading took place, is the weatherboarded building behind the lorry. The Bell, right, was an important coaching inn, and it still enjoys a high reputation. It dates from the 15th century. The bell on the sign bears the motto 'I call for the living, I toll for the dead, I scatter the lightning'.

Corringham, The Bull Inn c1950 C243005
Corringham still retains some old buildings. The Bull dates largely from the 17th century, though the wing on the right, with its projecting gable, is two centuries older. Like so many pubs around here, it has smuggling connections, being riddled with sliding panels, double doors and secret chambers. A weekly animal market used to be held outside.

**Corringham
Woodbrooke Way
c1955** C243044
These shops serve
an outlying part of
Corringham: they
are the usual mix of
grocer, newsagent
and hardware-shop.
The latter has a
wheelbarrow and
roller on display on
the pavement; there
is a weighing-machine
outside Galbraith's. The
car is a divided-screen
Morris Minor.

Corringham, Lampits Hill c1950 C243012
Corringham was a small, remote village before the coming of the oil-refineries: the petrol-station sign in the distance says it all. This parade was built in 1929. The pavement here is a jungle of Belisha beacons, old-fashioned street lamps, telegraph poles, A-boards, bus-stops, and an unusual white phone-box.

Fobbing, The White Lion Hotel c1955 F78002
The original core of the White Lion - to the left of the picture - is thought to date from the 15th century. Fobbing's moment of glory was in the past even then: a local labourer called Jack Straw had been one of the prime movers in the Peasants' Revolt of 1381. Chaucer mentions him in 'The Canterbury Tales' as a paradigm of noisiness: 'Jakke Straw...ne maden never shoutes half so shrille'. But then, Essex people were not known for going down without a fight.

Index

FRITH PRODUCTS & SERVICES

Francis Frith would doubtless be pleased to know that the pioneering publishing venture he started in 1860 still continues today. Over a hundred and forty years later, The Francis Frith Collection continues in the same innovative tradition and is now one of the foremost publishers of vintage photographs in the world. Some of the current activities include:

INTERIOR DECORATION

Today Frith's photographs can be seen framed and as giant wall murals in thousands of pubs, restaurants, hotels, banks, retail stores and other public buildings throughout the country. In every case they enhance the unique local atmosphere of the places they depict and provide reminders of gentler days in an increasingly busy and frenetic world.

PRODUCT PROMOTIONS

Frith products are used by many major companies to promote the sales of their own products or to reinforce their own history and heritage. Frith promotions have been used by Hovis bread, Courage beers, Scots Porage Oats, Colman's mustard, Cadbury's foods, Mellow Birds coffee, Dunhill pipe tobacco, Guinness, and Bulmer's Cider.

GENEALOGY AND FAMILY HISTORY

As the interest in family history and roots grows world-wide, more and more people are turning to Frith's photographs of Great Britain for images of the towns, villages and streets where their ancestors lived; and, of course, photographs of the churches and chapels where their ancestors were christened, married and buried are an essential part of every genealogy tree and family album.

FRITH PRODUCTS

All Frith photographs are available Framed or just as Mounted Prints and unmounted versions. These may be ordered from the address below. Other products available are - Calendars, Jigsaws, Canvas Prints, Mugs, Tea Towels, Tableware and local and prestige books.

THE INTERNET

Over several hundred thousand Frith photographs can be viewed and purchased on the internet through the Frith websites!

For more detailed information on Frith products, look at
www.francisfrith.com

See the complete list of Frith Books at: www.francisfrith.com
This web site is regularly updated with the latest list of publications from The Francis Frith Collection. If you wish to buy books relating to another part of the country that your local bookshop does not stock, you may purchase on-line.

For further information, trade, or author enquiries please contact us at the address below:
The Francis Frith Collection, 19 Kingsmead Business Park, Gillingham, Dorset SP8 5FB.
Tel: +44 (0)1722 716 376   Email: sales@francisfrith.co.uk

See Frith products on the internet at www.francisfrith.com

FREE PRINT OF YOUR CHOICE
CHOOSE A PHOTOGRAPH FROM THIS BOOK

+ POSTAGE

Mounted Print
Overall size 14 x 11 inches (355 x 280mm)

TO RECEIVE YOUR FREE PRINT

Choose any Frith photograph in this book

Simply complete the Voucher opposite and
return it with your payment (to cover postage
and handling) and we will print the photograph
of your choice in SEPIA (size 11 x 8 inches) and
supply it in a cream mount ready to frame
(overall size 14 x 11 inches).

Order additional Mounted Prints
at HALF PRICE - £19.00 each (normally £38.00)

If you would like to order more Frith prints
from this book, possibly as gifts for friends and
family, you can buy them at half price (with no
additional postage costs).

Have your Mounted Prints framed

For an extra £20.00 per print you can have your
mounted print(s) framed in an elegant polished
wood and gilt moulding, overall size
16 x 13 inches (no additional postage required).

IMPORTANT!

❶ Please note: aerial photographs and photographs
with a reference number starting with a "Z" are not Frith
photographs and cannot be supplied under this offer.

❷ Offer valid for delivery to one UK address only.

❸ These special prices are only available if you use this
form to order. You must use the ORIGINAL VOUCHER on
this page (no copies permitted). We can only despatch
to one UK address.

❹ This offer cannot be combined with any other offer.

As a customer your name & address will be stored by Frith but not sold or rented
to third parties. Your data will be used for the purpose of this promotion only.

Send completed Voucher form to:

**The Francis Frith Collection,
19 Kingsmead Business Park, Gillingham,
Dorset SP8 5FB**

Voucher for **FREE** and Reduced Price *Frith Prints*

*Please do not photocopy this voucher. Only the original is valid,
so please fill it in, cut it out and return it to us with your order.*

Picture ref no	Page no	Qty	Mounted @ £19.00	Framed + £20.00	Total Cost £
		1	Free of charge*	£	£
			£19.00	£	£
			£19.00	£	£
			£19.00	£	£
			£19.00	£	£
			£19.00	£	£

*Please allow 28 days
for delivery.
Offer available to one
UK address only*

* Post & handling	£3.80
Total Order Cost	£

Title of this book . . . .

I enclose a cheque/postal order for £ . . . .

made payable to 'The Francis Frith Collection'

OR please debit my Mastercard / Visa / Maestro card,
details below

Card Number:

Issue No (Maestro only):   Valid from (Maestro):

Card Security Number: Expires:

Signature:

Name Mr/Mrs/Ms . . . .

Address . . . .

. . . .

. . . .

. . . . Postcode . . . .

Daytime Tel No . . . .

Email . . . .

Valid to 31/12/20

Free Print – see overleaf

Can you help us with information about any of the Frith photographs in this book?

We are gradually compiling an historical record for each of the photographs in the Frith archive. It is always fascinating to find out the names of the people shown in the pictures, as well as insights into the shops, buildings and other features depicted.

If you recognize anyone in the photographs in this book, or if you have information not already included in the author's caption, do let us know. We would love to hear from you, and will try to publish it in future books or articles.

An Invitation from The Francis Frith Collection to Share Your Memories

The 'Share Your Memories' feature of our website allows members of the public to add personal memories relating to the places featured in our photographs, or comment on others already added. Seeing a place from your past can rekindle forgotten or long held memories. Why not visit the website, find photographs of places you know well and add YOUR story for others to read and enjoy? We would love to hear from you!

www.francisfrith.com/memories

Our production team

Frith books are produced by a small dedicated team at offices near Salisbury. Most have worked with the Frith Collection for many years. All have in common one quality: they have a passion for the Frith Collection.

Frith Books and Gifts

We have a wide range of books and gifts available on our website utilising our photographic archive, many of which can be individually personalised.

www.francisfrith.com